THE
POLITICAL
VISIONARY

ANDRE THOMAS

GREATNESS
PUBLISHING

www.ignitingworldchangers.org

Published by Greatness Publishing, Ontario, Canada

Cover Design and formatting by Farouk Roberts, Brands & Love Creative
www.brandsnlove.com

Photos by Natalie Ali

Library and Archives Canada
ISBN 978-1-927579-04-6

ACKNOWLEDGMENTS

Special thanks go to:

Nancy Dickerson for editing

Farouk J. Roberts for formatting

Natalie Ali for photos

I dedicate this book to Nina D. Jackson.
Your entry into my life has given me
wings to fly high where I belong.

Thank You

CONTENTS

INTRODUCTION

Over the years, I have studied political leaders who have achieved transformational results through service. I have found among their leadership styles six common ingredients – six "pillars" that undergird their transformational political careers. In this book, I offer them to you.

This book is not about the presentation of a "successful" political governance model accompanied by a suggestion that it must be adapted by all nations to bring growth through a one-size-fits-all solution. This book is about the empowerment of practicing and aspiring political leaders *like yourself.*

It will help you:

1. Cultivate characteristics within yourself and your administration that will create a culturally intelligent model of governance.
2. Develop a model specifically suited to your town, city, region or nation, with a hope of producing a safe and prosperous society.

You will find the wisdom in this book to be motivational, principle-centered, and illustrated with historical examples. It is designed to **ignite innovation in a new generation of political leaders.**

It is divided into six sections:

1. Political Vision

2. Leadership Character
3. Political Strategy
4. Sound Political Judgment
5. Ability to Build Critical Mass of Passionate and Able People
6. Cultural Intelligence

It is a fundamental truth that **the challenges of a generation will *never be greater* than the ideas and solutions within the people born into that generation.**

WHAT IS LEADERSHIP?

Leadership at its highest level is not a science, but an art form. It involves

1. Thinking visionary thoughts;
2. Applying leadership principles;
3. Taking creative steps in culturally relevant ways to actualize your vision;

The culture and historical context of a situation in one nation usually differs from that of another. The way you accomplish a transformational vision in each nation, therefore, differs. In each case it will depend on the way you lead and what you do to ignite the passion and deploy the skill of people. However, it often takes *innovative leadership* to bring workable ideas and solutions from concept to reality.

WHAT IS INNOVATIVE LEADERSHIP?

Innovation is *the* creative force in the human race that cuts a path to new and better levels of existence. Innovation is not limited to technology, science or medicine; it extends to areas like business and politics.

Innovation is thinking outside the box of history to find new ways to solve old problems and challenges.

When the principles of innovation in leadership are applied to politics in a culturally intelligent way, new and exciting solutions are created. I have come to believe that **the greatness of a people will never emerge until the greatness of its business, educational, spiritual, and political leaders emerge.** Innovative political leadership is the spark that ignites the greatness of our cities and regions as we face uncertain economic times. It brings economic and social transformation.

Political transformation occurs when there is a willing leader, a critical mass of willing and able citizens and favorable circumstances.

This is not just about policy. It is about

- Igniting innovation among political visionaries of your generation;
- Examining innovative political leadership and the variables that affect political decision-making.

For instance, when you come into office, you are dealt a hand by fate in four areas that are outside of your control:

- The present culture of your town, city or nation;
- The geography of your town, city or nation;
- The circumstances in which your town, city or nation finds itself;
- The legacy inherited from your predecessor.

Within your control lie the wisdom and ability to take what you have inherited and through a series of sequential steps, create what you envision. This section will help you identify and utilize *leadership wisdom.*

This exercise will involve the use of the following cognitive functions:
1. ☐ Reflective thinking
2. ☐ Possibility thinking
3. ☐ Bottom-line thinking
4. ☐ Reality thinking
5. ☐ Creative thinking
6. ☐ Strategic thinking

As you work through the content and exercises of this b o o k, let them inspire and ignite *you* to become **a transformational political leader!**

CHAPTER ONE

POLITICAL VISIONARIES

True political visionaries are a rare breed. They are shapers of the destinies of nations through politics. Their focus is three-fold:

1. **Governance, which** utilizes government positively to impact and improve the life of its citizens;
2. **Campaigning** with the aim of getting into, and staying in political office.
3. **Policy Creation** with formulates and develops polices for national advancement and protection.

There are two types of political visionaries:

1. **Habitual leaders** are people who have a natural inclination to lead in almost any circumstance.
2. **Situational leaders** are people whose leadership genius only emerges when they find themselves by design or accident in a situation that matches their passion, gifting, intelligence and skill sets.

Just like it takes a genetic gift to run 100 meters in less than ten seconds, it also takes a genetic gift to positively transform a town, city or nation through political leadership.

I define politics and political leadership thus:

POLITICAL VISIONARIES

- **Politics** is the art or science of governing a country's internal and external relations.

- **Political leadership** is the art of igniting the passion, deploying the skills and rallying the resources of a people to accomplish a political
vision.

In order to establish a platform of understanding, I will define the words *vision*, and *political visionary*.

- **A vision** is a clear mental portrait of a preferred future.

- **A political visionary** is a person who possesses both a clear, compelling mental portrait of the potential of a town, city or nation,
and the innate potential to take that vision from concept to reality.

A person who has a vision for the potential of the city, but does not have innate potential to bring it to pass, is a *political dreamer*! There are many political dreamers in office. The threshold of the ability of political visionaries is ordered in ranks. It comes in measures that determine a visionary's capacity to lead. Some don't have the gifting to aspire beyond a certain level. The threshold of their ability may only be for governing a village. For others it may be for a town, a city, a region, or a nation.

Thresholds of ability in leaders vary according to their giftings. Great political visionaries may be gifted for the roles of mayors, ministers of parliament, governors, leaders within political parties and presidents. Conversely, good political leaders with great track records can fail overnight. From being champions of the people, they can fall and be perceived as villains because they were thrust into a political office that was higher than their capacity to govern.
A hypothetical example may be that of a good political leader who is given the portfolio of a minister of health. He was a great leader of his

constituency of half a million, but the new assignment is beyond his ability.

He does not have the innate giftings to manage the health affairs of the country.

THE VALUE OF GREAT POLITICAL LEADERSHIP

In the school of political governance we encounter the good, the bad and the ugly.

Good political governance provides protection for the citizens of a region and creates conditions that make it easy for people to experience social peace, economic empowerment and educational achievement. The object of good political governance is to release the potential of a town, city, region or nation. Good political leaders govern for the emergence and advancement of their people in such a way that their greatness and potential emerge.

Bad political governance occurs when the citizens of a region are not adequately protected and when leaders are not proactive in creating conditions of social peace, economic empowerment or educational advancement for their people. They let things be.

Ugly political governance is the promotion of ignorance. It occurs when innocent citizens of a region are victimized and when leaders, for selfish purposes, intentionally create social strife, economic disenfranchisement and the advancement of policies that promote the ignorance of the people.

UNDERSTANDING YOUR INNATE POLITICAL STRENGTHS

Very few political visionaries, if any, have equally high innate strength in both campaigning and governance. Generally one is stronger than the other.

In this section we have provided personal application questions that will help you assess your innate qualities and help you analyze how they apply to your political office. Your understanding of yourself will be enhanced if you can consult with a trusted associate or colleague concerning your responses.

Personal Application

1. On a scale of one to ten, assess your innate campaigning ability.

Low	1	2	3	4	5	6	7	8	9	10	High

2. On a scale of one to ten, assess your innate governance ability.

Low	1	2	3	4	5	6	7	8	9	10	High

3. Are you a habitual or situational leader? Why do you think so?

_____

_____

_____

_____

_____

_____

CHALLENGES TO POLITICAL LEADERSHIP

In the present global environment, political leadership is one of the most demanding leadership roles in the world. Every political leader faces opportunities and challenges in four areas:

1. Culture of the nation
2. Regional geography
3. Regional circumstances
4. :Legacy of the predecessor

1.   The Culture of the Nation

Culture encompasses all the ways of life of a population, including its arts, beliefs and institutions that are passed down from generation to generation. The culture, or national character of a nation, can favour or hinder rapid development. If your nation's cultural values include discipline and hard work, then your job is to unleash the strengths of the culture for national development. If your nation's cultural character includes corruption and violence, to succeed you must lead a cultural re-engineering movement. It goes without saying that cultural re-engineering is more difficult than unleashing the latent force of a growth-friendly society.

Personal Application

How would you describe the political culture of the region you aspire to lead?

_____

_____

_____

_____

_____

_____

_____

_____

_____

_____

_____

How would you describe the economic culture of the region you aspire to lead?

_____

_____

_____

_____

_____

_____

_____

_____

_____

_____

How would you describe the social culture of the region you aspire to lead?

_____

_____

_____

_____

_____

_____

_____

_____

_____

_____

_____

How would you describe the religious culture of the region you aspire to lead?

_____

_____

_____

_____

_____

_____

_____

_____

_____

_____

2. Regional Geography

Geography matters. The inherent wealth and challenges of the geography of a region must be understood by every political leader. It creates a unique set of opportunities and challenges.

Some regions, like Florida and the Caribbean, face challenges from hurricanes and yet have great opportunities for tourism. Some regions, like Texas and Nigeria, are rich in mineral resources. Other regions, like Barbados have no mineral resources at all.

Some regions, like Chad, are landlocked and susceptible to drought. Others, like the United Kingdom, have consistent rainfall and are surrounded by water.

Personal Application

Your responses will help you understand the geographical opportunities and challenges of your region.

What types of geographical opportunities and wealth are there in your region? Are they being utilized?

_____

_____

_____

_____

_____

_____

_____

_____

_____

_____

_____

What are the untapped resources and opportunities of your region?

_____

_____

_____

_____

_____

_____

_____

_____

_____

What challenges are inherent in your geographical region?

_____

_____

_____

_____

_____

_____

_____

_____

_____

_____

_____

_____

3. Regional circumstances

The word *circumstance* comes from the two words, *circle* and *stand*. It literally means, *the circle of events in which you stand*. The circle of global, regional and domestic events in which your region stands has a direct impact on your ability to execute your vision.

Personal Application

Your responses will help you understand the circle of events in which your region stands.

Every mayor of New York will face a significant security challenge from terrorism, while the mayor of Bulacan, Philippines, does not have those considerations.

What are the present security circumstances in your region?

_____

_____

_____

_____

_____

_____

_____

_____

_____

_____

What are the present economic events affecting your region?

_____

_____

_____

_____

_____

_____

_____

_____

_____

_____

_____

What are the present social events affecting your region?

_____

_____

_____

_____

_____

_____

_____

_____

_____

_____

_____

What are the present political events affecting your region?

_____

_____

_____

_____

_____

_____

_____

_____

_____

_____

_____

What are the present religious beliefs influencing your region?

_____

_____

_____

_____

_____

_____

_____

_____

_____

_____

_____

4. Regional legacy

Legacy matters. If you assume office in a failed state like Afghanistan,
or a growing economy like Brazil, your opportunities and challenges
will differ.

Personal Application

What is the general public perception of the political regional legacy you will inherit?

_____

_____

_____

_____

_____

_____

_____

_____

_____

_____

What is the foreign relations legacy you will inherit?

_____

_____

_____

_____

_____

_____

_____

_____

_____

_____

_____

What is the security legacy you will inherit?

_____

_____

_____

_____

_____

_____

_____

_____

_____

_____

What is the financial legacy you will inherit?

_____

_____

_____

_____

_____

_____

_____

_____

_____

_____

_____

_____

A GREAT POLITICAL VISIONARY

Against the backdrop of regional culture, geography, circumstances and legacy, the political visionary enters, sees what *is* and what *can be*, mobilizes resources and charts a course to achieve what *must be*.

Acclaimed as the father of Barbados' independence, Errol Walton Barrow was born in the parish of St. Lucy on January 21,1920. A founding member of the Democratic Labour Party, Barrow swept to power as premier in 1961 and held that position until 1966. He became Barbados' first Prime Minister when his party won the elections in 1966 to 1976 and again in 1985 to 1987, and took the island into independence from Britain. Among his many great accomplishments, the visionary course he set for Barbados and the national identity he infused into the people, stand out. It is said he found a collection of villages and left it a proud country.

Former Prime Minister Owen Arthur of Barbados, in a 2007 speech honoring the legacy of Errol Barrow, eloquently speaks about his visionary legacy in these words:

Mr. Barrow was, first and foremost, driven by a passion to make the

Barbadian people great, not only insofar as the region was concerned, but also in the family of nations, both developing and developed. He possessed an unwavering dedication to a vision of world-class status for the Caribbean region's most industrious small nation. As early as 1950 he visualized the possibility of Barbados becoming a world-class society. Thus, this dedicated nationalist let down his bucket in Barbados of the 1950s, first as a lieutenant to the venerable Sir Grantley Adams, then striking out on his own and creating his own mass-based political force – the Democratic Labor Party. The question may be asked – what distinguished the Right Excellent Errol Barrow from other Barbadian (and Caribbean) leaders of his era? Let me identify five and possibly six areas in which Mr. Barrow so acquitted himself as to be regarded by most people as the "father of modern Barbados."

Firstly, Mr. Barrow was a crusader on behalf of the common man. His care and concern for our working class was almost legendary. His was a lifelong campaigner to eliminate poverty and wretchedness from Barbados. Then there is Barrow the great revolutionary and father of independence. Many thousands of words have been written and spoken of his bold decision in 1965 to press for constitutional independence for this island. Mr. Barrow correctly gauged the eagerness and enthusiasm of the Barbadian masses for their freedom from Britain's imperial embrace and led us to that glorious date with destiny on the 30th day of November 1966.

Time has not diminished nor dimmed the luster of that wonderful occasion, nor have events conspired to make our recollections of November 1966 bitter ones. To the contrary, the new nation which he ushered in that year is now standing near the threshold of First World status and is currently pressing for acceptance as a world-class society. Thirdly, we must take note of Errol Barrow the visionary educator – the man who completed the Grantley Adams program of liberating education

17

from the clutches of class and racial prejudices. We laud and magnify his name whenever our children write the 11-plus Common Entrance Examination each year and whenever they contentedly eat their school meals each school-day. We continue to express our admiration for the man who introduced the pioneering concept of the Barbados Community College in 1968, and we stand in awe when we remember that he single-handedly introduced University education to Barbados in 1963 with the opening of what was to become the Cave Hill Campus. Fourthly, the Right Excellent

Mr. Barrow was a builder. All around us we can see examples of his work. There is the Treasury Building, the First National Insurance Building, the Middle Income Housing developments of the 1960s and the 1970s; the Industrial Estates, the expansion to the Airport and the Seaport and a number of schools such as Ellerslie, Parkinson Secondary and St Lucy Secondary. Mr. Barrow's magnanimity and passion for harmony also inspire us with respect and admiration. This is the fifth area of glorious achievement during his term of office, 1961 to 1987 and particularly after

1966, when several voices questioned the wisdom of his decision to take Barbados into Independence alone. Mr. Barrow assumed the mantle of a statesman and held out the "olive branch" to the former plantation and commercial elite who had ruled Barbados up to the 1940s. To them he became the harbinger of democracy, progress, harmony and cooperation. He practiced the politics of inclusiveness long before it became a total force in the 21st century, making whites, Jews, Muslims, Hindus and other ethnic minorities in this society feel comfortable and safe. At the same time he overturned the culture of racial discrimination and secured for all Barbadians their fundamental rights. To all Barbadians he was "the Great Reconciler."

There is a sixth arena in which he shone like a beacon of progressiveness and cooperation – the pertinent sphere of regional integration. It is an important aspect of the traditions of Barbadian leaders, that a significant part of their lifework should be dedicated to the cause of advancing Caribbean unity. No tribute to this National Hero and Caribbean man would be complete without a generous mention of his valiant efforts to promote cooperation among Britain's former colonies in the Caribbean. Along with Eric Williams and Vere Bird, he was one of the Founding Fathers of CARIFTA in 1965. With Manley, Williams and Burnham, he was at the founding of CARICOM in 1973. "

This transformational political leader laid the foundation and set the course for significant development in Barbados and its present ranking of 31 on the United Nations Development Program Human Index. **You can do the same.**

CHAPTER TWO

CREATING A VISION

Political vision is a clear, compelling mental portrait of what the people of a region can achieve and possess if they continue developing themselves and maximizing their regional resources.

Political vision is the root of all great political leadership. I believe strongly that a leader is hindered in their ability to lead a town, city and nation if they don't have a clear, compelling political vision that can be articulated to their constituents. Sometimes people with strong management abilities are placed in leadership positions where the skill-set required to succeed is different from what is required from management. They will not be able to fulfill a leadership position adequately.

MANAGERS AND LEADERS

Leaders differ from managers. Leaders influence people to follow direction and shape tomorrow with ideas. Managers steward resources to meet preset objectives. In the arena of politics, managers effectively and efficiently manage resources to meet pre-existing regional goals. Political managers can be *followers* of a transformational leader, however their gift-mix cannot engineer political transformation. They can work and inherit the legacy of a transformational leader and build on his achievements, but they do not have the innate ability for shaping tomorrow with political ideas.

Personal Application

Do you consider yourself naturally more gifted in the stewardship of existing resources and their management in order to meet specific objectives, or do you see yourself as a leader who influences people and shapes tomorrow with political ideas?

Indicate why you have these perceptions about yourself:

_____

_____

_____

_____

_____

_____

_____

_____

_____

_____

_____

_____

DEVELOPING A REGIONAL POLITICAL VISION

The process of developing a regional political vision is a journey. It requires the involvement of stakeholders within the region in a formal or informal way.

It is founded on the following:

1. Regional character

The analysis of the strengths and weaknesses of the people of a region is critical in developing a regional political vision. Personal character, organizational character and regional character must be considered. Every regional culture has strengths and weaknesses and every people-group has inherent shared gifts and inadequacies. A regional political vision must build on people's strengths while taking into account their weaknesses.

Personal Application

List the strengths of the collective culture and the people groups within your region.

_____

_____

_____

_____

_____

_____

_____

_____

_____

_____

_____

List the weaknesses of the collective culture and the people groups within your region.

_____

_____

_____

_____

_____

_____

_____

_____

_____

_____

_____

2. Resources of the Region

The resources of its people are a nation's greatest asset. Other resources such as minerals, natural beauty, geography, and so on, must be thoroughly analyzed for their potential value to the region and to the rest of the world. In the Caribbean, one of the greatest resources is scenic beauty. The sun, sea and sand have been marketed, have generated billions of dollars in revenue and have created thousands of jobs.

Personal Application

List the natural resources of your region.

_____

_____

_____

_____

_____

_____

_____

_____

_____

_____

_____

3. Regional Contribution

The world is a large marketplace and money is the medium of exchange of goods and services. If a region has no significant goods or services to offer the world, it will remain, or become poor. The region's goods and services that can add value to the world must be thoroughly analyzed, developed, marketed and sold with excellence to create a sustainable revenue stream for the region.

Every nation has something to offer the world that will bring it distinction.

Personal Application

What are the existing goods and services that your region contributes to the world? Can they be further developed?

_____

_____

_____

_____

_____

_____

_____

_____

_____

_____

_____

What are the goods and services that can be developed in your region to create revenue?

_____

_____

_____

_____

_____

_____

_____

_____

_____

_____

_____

THE ROLE OF THINK TANKS IN DEVELOPING REGIONS

Think tanks are very important, but useless unless political leaders respect them. **People who do not take time to think become victims of the opinions of others.** Think tanks with local, national and international reach are essential in adding value to the process of developing a regional vision and creating a strategy for its fulfillment.

Different schools of thought are an attribute of political maturity. Competing homemade think tanks that drive discussion concerning the strategy, policies and future of the region are good.
Developing regions are in desperate need of think tanks at every rank of political leadership.

The womb of a region's thinking will either deliver its potential, or abort it.

26

DEVELOPING A REGIONAL VISION

The process of developing a regional political vision has an end point. At that point, the vision is crystallized, made known to the people, and everything in the administration must now be aligned for the one purpose of achieving that vision. To assist the aspiring political visionary, here is a summary of steps involved in developing a political vision:

1. Identify the strengths and weaknesses of the regional culture.
2. Identify the marketable resources of the region.
3. Identify the problems in the world that the region can solve by producing goods or services at a profit.
4. Use the research gathered in steps one, two and three to create your political vision for the region.
5. Communicate the vision to young and old during your campaign process. If you are already in political office, give every citizen access to the vision and help them understand it.
6. Align every arm of government with the according to the vision
7. Place people with the required passion, competence and character in key areas to oversee the execution of the vision. The realization of regional visions requires a critical mass of people with passionate competence and integrity.
8. Allocate resources and draw up strategies and policies to achieve the vision.
9. As the primary political leader, you and your core team must now navigate the journey from the inception of the vision to its translation into reality.

Personal Application

Create a political vision for your constituents.

_____

_____

_____

_____

_____

_____

_____

_____

_____

_____

_____

_____

_____

_____

_____

_____

_____

_____

_____

CHAPTER THREE

LEADERSHIP CHARACTER

CHARACTER ATTRIBUTES OF TRANSFORMATIONAL POLITICAL LEADERS

The role of the transformational political leader is not for the weak and faint at heart. It is for the principled, centered, culturally smart, disciplined, courageous, service driven, politically savvy and emotionally intelligent individual.

FIFTEEN ATTRIBUTES OF GREAT POLITICAL VISIONARIES

1. Service-driven: Service is the process of adding value to others.

Great political visionaries are service-driven. They are motivated by serving and leading their regions into a better future. They are passionate about making a contribution to their people.

They have discovered that serving a cause greater than their selves gives fulfillment to life.

When we connect ourselves to causes that outlast our lives, our highest and best attributes surface

Selfishness-driven: To be service-driven is the opposite of being selfish. When the focus of political leadership is *Me, Myself and I*, the future of a region is bleak.

Political selfishness is the art of using political office to profit yourself and your cronies at the expense of the people you are supposed to be serving. Political selfishness is the tomb of the potential of a people and the killer of regional dreams.

Personal Application

Are you service-driven or selfishness-driven? On a scale of one to ten, assess the strength of the attribute of service in your life. To eliminate "blind spots," I suggest you also ask your friends or love ones to score you for this attribute. They will tell you the truth.

Circle the score you (and your closest associates) a s s i g n yourself selfishness:

Service

Low	1	2	3	4	5	6	7	8	9	10	High

2. **Courage - Courage is the ability to take a determined course of action in the presence of hostility and adversity.**

The journey of transformational leadership is a journey of courage. This quality must be the backbone of every political leader. Courage is required to cast a new vision for the direction of your region. Courage is required to deal swiftly with enemies of the progress of the state.

Courage is required to allow your legal, political opposition to express their views freely in true democratic style without your illegal and unethical reprisals. Courage is required to speak directly and truthfully to the people about the state of your region. Courage is required to choose the best ethical minds to serve in your administration even if they don't always agree with your policies. Courage is required when it is necessary to order lethal force to combat situations that threaten to sabotage regional progress.

Personal Application

On a scale of one to ten, assess the strength of courage in your life. To eliminate "blind spots," I suggest you also ask your friends or love ones to score you on this attribute. They will tell you the truth.

Circle the score you (and your closest associates) assign yourself.

Low	1	2	3	4	5	6	7	8	9	10	High

3. Principle-centeredness

A principle-centered person is one who has a set of core values that frames the way they see the world and helps them make decisions. Great political leaders are principle-centered.

People without non-negotiable guiding principles become victims of present expediency that sabotages future prosperity.
Personal Application

31

On a scale of one to ten, assess the strength of principle-centeredness in your life. To eliminate "blind spots," I suggest you also ask your friends or love ones to score you on this attribute. They will tell you the truth.

Circle the score you (and your closest associates) assign yourself.

Low	1	2	3	4	5	6	7	8	9	10	High

4. Emotional security

The size of your challenges, not your feelings of insecurity, must dictate the size and ability of your team. Insecurity in leaders is a curse.

- ☐ It sabotages their ability to build strong teams with the best and brightest minds in their region.
- ☐ It causes them to surround themselves with yes-people who are too timid to challenge them, or too intellectually challenged to understand the ramifications of inept political governance.

Emotionally secure people manage their emotions. They are self-aware, people-aware, have an ability to empathize, and seldom allow their emotions to hijack their common sense and intellect.

Personal Application

On a scale of one to ten, assess your emotional security. To eliminate "blind spots," I suggest you also ask your friends or loved ones to score you on this attribute. They will tell you the truth.

Circle the score you (and your closest associates) assign yourself.

Low	1	2	3	4	5	6	7	8	9	10	High

5. Humble confidence

Humility is your recognition of your own weaknesses, inabilities and vulnerabilities.

Confidence is your recognition and bold expression of your own strengths, abilities and gifts.

Both must live side by side in a great leader. A great leader must know his limitations and his strengths. He must promote his weakness and magnify his abilities. He must be both a lion and a lamb. This is the character paradox of great leadership in every human endeavor.

Personal Application

a. On a scale of one to ten assess the strength of humility in your life. To eliminate blind spots, I suggest you ask your friends or loved ones to score you on this attribute.

Circle the score you (and your closest associates) assign yourself.

Low	1	2	3	4	5	6	7	8	9	10	High

b.   On a scale of one to ten, assess the strength of confidence in your life. To eliminate "blind spots," I suggest you also ask your friends or loved ones to score you on this attribute. They will tell you the truth.

Circle the score you (and your closest associates) assign yourself.

Low	1	2	3	4	5	6	7	8	9	10	High

6. Integrity

A person of integrity is the same in their public life as they are in their private life.

To have integrity is to be the same in the shadows as in the light. It is to be "one." It means that your personal life and your public life are integrated. A person of integrity is not without *flaws. They are* without *hypocrisy*. Integrity creates the currency of trust required to mobilize a people to take huge political and economic leaps forward. A lack of integrity will eventually undermine the trust of people around you. When trust is gone, transformational leadership is impossible.

Personal Application

On a scale of one to ten, assess the strength of integrity in your life. To eliminate "blind spots," I suggest you also ask your friends or loved ones to score you on this attribute. They will tell you the truth.
Circle the score you (and your closest associates) assign yourself.

Low	1	2	3	4	5	6	7	8	9	10	High

7. Focus

Focus is the ability to concentrate on the required priorities in order to acquire what you desire. Good political leaders do not become victims of small, screaming problems. They focus on the big picture and the critical priorities that are required to accomplish their regional vision. They are mission-centered and focused in their personal lives, administration and regional policies.

Personal Application

On a scale of one to ten, assess the strength of focus in your life. To eliminate "blind spots," I suggest you also ask your friends or loved ones to score you on this attribute. They will tell you the truth.

Circle the score you (and your closest associates) assign yourself.

Low	1	2	3	4	5	6	7	8	9	10	High

8. Discipline

Discipline is doing what is required consistently, in and out of season, to acquire what you desire. A great man said that discipline is the soul of an army. It makes small numbers formidable and gives strength to all. Disciplined leaders create disciplined administrations that create disciplined regions that achieve their potential. **Transformational political leadership is impossible without discipline.**

Personal Application

On a scale of one to ten, assess the strength of discipline in your life. To eliminate "blind spots," I suggest you also ask your friends or loved ones to

Circle the score you (and your closest associates) assign yourself.

Low	1	2	3	4	5	6	7	8	9	10	High

9. Passion

Passion is a fiery, strong emotion that propels transformational leaders to action.

Passion distinguishes between two types of political interest:
- that of political achievers
- and that of political commentators

Passion is an indispensable quality of great political achievers. Political achievers analyze regional problems. Their passion to solve these problems propels them into the arena of regional life. Political commentators are proficient in analyzing and discussing regional and national problems, but they do not get involved in creating solutions.

The truly passionate cannot just commentate.

Personal Application

On a scale of one to ten, assess the strength of passion in your life. To eliminate "blind spots," I suggest you also ask your friends or loved ones to
score you on this attribute. They will tell you the truth.

Low	1	2	3	4	5	6	7	8	9	10	High

Circle the score you (and your closest associates) assign yourself.

Low	1	2	3	4	5	6	7	8	9	10	High

10. Innovation

Innovation is the ability to create new solutions for old problems. Innovation finds new ways of tackling old issues. It thinks *outside* the box of history and reaches into the realm of human possibility to bring a solution that *makes* history. **Current global problems require innovative political leaders who stand on the achievements of history, learn wisdom from the failures of history and do not become prisoners of history.** Innovation in the primary political leader is not enough to bring transformation in a region. Innovators are required throughout the administration to lift us above shallow thinking and shape the future with ideas. An innovative administration will be full of fresh, workable ideas to take nations, regions, cities and towns forward.

The motto of an innovator: **There always is a way, even if it has not yet been discovered.**

Personal Application

On a scale of one to ten, assess the strength of innovation in your life. To eliminate "blind spots," I suggest you also ask your friends or loved ones to score you on this attribute. They will tell you the truth.

Circle the score you (and your closest associates) assign yourself.

Low	1	2	3	4	5	6	7	8	9	10	High

11. Love for One's Country

Love is a deep-seated care for the interests of another that propels an individual to action.
The opposite of love is selfishness. Love for one's country is an indispensable quality of great political leadership. Love for one's country burns with volcanic fervor in the heart of transformational political leaders. It propels them into bold, daring, uplifting transformational actions.

Personal Application

On a scale of one to ten, assess the strength of your love for your country. To eliminate "blind spots," I suggest you also ask your friends or loved ones to score you on this attribute. They will tell you the truth.

Circle the score you (and your closest associates) assign yourself.

Low	1	2	3	4	5	6	7	8	9	10	High

12. Inner political radar

Inner political radar is the ability of transformational leaders to discern and read people and situations, and intuitively identify imminent danger in their sphere of influence before the danger fully manifests. Throughout the ages, all great transformational leaders have possessed powerful inner political radar. Whether it is genetic or developed, I'm not sure. I do know it can literally be a life saver and it protects the transformation as it occurs. An inner political radar is not the result of suspicion, but it is the ability to unemotionally read positive and negative visible and invisible data about people and events.

Personal Application

On a scale of one to ten, assess the strength of inner political radar in your life. To eliminate "blind spots," I suggest you also ask your friends or love ones to score you on this attribute. They will tell you the truth.

Circle the score you (and your closest associates) assign yourself.

Low	1	2	3	4	5	6	7	8	9	10	High

13. Persuasive Communicator

A persuasive communicator has the ability to promote his/her ideas, solutions and character effectively. This ability undergirds all transformational political leaders. They have a healthy dose of persuasive power and are great at "selling" what they can do for their region and what their region can do for the world.

Personal Application

On a scale of one to ten, assess the strength of persuasion in your life. To eliminate "blind spots," I suggest you also ask your friends or loved ones to score you on this attribute. They will tell you the truth.

Circle the score you (and your closest associates) assign yourself.

Low	1	2	3	4	5	6	7	8	9	10	High

14. Great team builder

Great team builders have the ability to build teams that protect their weaknesses and possess the passion, skill, loyalty, courage and intelligence to implement transformation in a nation, city or town.

While there are no perfect leaders, leaders can have perfect teams. The mastery of building teams that can engineer transformation in a town, city or region is a great aptitude for a political visionary to have in his/her skill set.

Personal Application

On a scale of one to ten, assess your ability to build great teams. To eliminate "blind spots," I suggest you also ask your friends or loved ones to score you on this attribute. They will tell you the truth.

Circle the score you (and your closest associates) assign yourself.

Low	1	2	3	4	5	6	7	8	9	10	High

15. Ability to connect with constituents

Transformational leaders have mastered the skill of using language that fits the situation at hand. The intellects of transformational political leaders are usually developed to higher degrees than those of the people- groups they lead. They are, however, able to connect with their constituents using language that motivates them to join their cause, or to launch a revolution.

Personal Application

On a scale of one to ten, assess your ability to connect with constituents. To eliminate "blind spots," I suggest you also ask your friends or love ones to score you on this attribute. They will tell you the truth.

Circle the score you (and your closest associates) assign yourself.

Low	1	2	3	4	5	6	7	8	9	10	High

INSPIRATIONAL STORIES
OF

Transformational Leaders

Nelson Mandela: *The bridge builder of South Africa.*

Few political leaders embody the character traits of a transformational leader like Nelson Mandela. Monarchs and presidents celebrate his words, celebrities crave to be in his presence, and the world's multitudes gather to hear his wisdom. They do so for one reason – the nature of his character. His character inspires the world to follow him and underpins the intellect that navigated South Africa from the brink of a social holocaust to a path of growing social cohesion and economic progress.

Nelson Rolihlahla Mandela was born July 18, 1918. He was the first president of South Africa to be elected in fully representative democratic elections. Before his presidency, Mandela was an anti-apartheid activist and leader of the African National Congress (ANC) and its armed wing, *Umkhonto we Sizwe*. He spent 27 years in prison, much of the time on Robben Island, on convictions for crimes that included sabotage, committed while he spearheaded the struggle against apartheid. Among opponents of apartheid in South Africa and internationally, he became a symbol of freedom and equality. The apartheid government, and nations sympathetic to it, condemned him and the ANC as communists and terrorists. Following his release from prison on February 11, 1990, his switch to a policy of reconciliation and negotiation helped lead the transition to multi-racial democracy in South Africa.

Since the end of apartheid, he has been widely praised and celebrated, even by former opponents. Mandela has received more than 100 awards over four decades, most notably the Nobel Peace Prize in 1993.

CHAPTER FOUR

NATIONAL STRATEGY

DEVELOPING A REGIONAL STRATEGY

Strategy is a sequential plan that takes you from your current reality to the realization of a desired future. Through strategy people, organizations and nations secure a great tomorrow.

Strategy is vital to accomplishing a regional vision. It is rooted in three foundational factors:

- a clear vision and defined objectives
- an understanding of one's current reality
- a sequential plan

Where a defined strategy is lacking, failure is inevitable. Failure occurs when people attempt to accomplish a demanding vision without a clearly thought-out sequential plan of action that reflects reality. A lack of strategy is often the undoing of sincere political leaders and their administrations.

REGIONAL VISION AND OBJECTIVES

A good regional strategy is built from a clear image of a desired

achievable future and from strategic objectives.

The strategic objectives of good governance
are:

- protection of citizens and national borders
- social peace and stability
- economic empowerment of the masses
- educational advancement of the masses

Strategic political navigation requires a political leader to act as a ship's captain – to plot a course through the rough seas and stormy weather of social strife, economic challenges and military conflict toward the realization of the vision, while also creating conditions for citizens to experience social peace, upward economic mobility and educational advancement during the transition.

UNDERSTANDING CURRENT REALITY

The process of understanding the current reality of a region involves thorough analysis of certain variables. The following questions will help you identify these variables within your sphere of political influence.

Personal Application

1. What plans are workable within the culture you represent?

_____

_____

_____

_____

_____

_____

_____

_____

_____

_____

_____

_____

2. What threat level does your region experience from internal and external
adversaries?

_____

_____

_____

_____

_____

_____

_____

_____

_____

_____

_____

_____

3. What is the actual level of social peace between ethnic groups
and religions in your region?

_____

_____

_____

_____

_____

_____

_____

_____

_____

_____

4. What is the level of ability of ordinary citizens in your region to
find work, own a home and finance family dreams.

_____

_____

_____

_____

_____

_____

_____

_____

_____

_____

5. What is the level of ability of ordinary citizens in your region to access capital to finance their dreams?

_____

_____

_____

_____

_____

_____

_____

_____

_____

_____

6. What is the level of the rule of law, separation of powers, and the protection of the basic liberties of speech, assembly, religion, and property rights in your region?

_____

_____

_____

_____

_____

_____

_____

_____

_____

_____

_____

7. What is the level of competitiveness of the population of your region in the global economy?

_____

_____

_____

_____

_____

_____

_____

_____

_____

_____

_____

A SEQUENTIAL PLAN

A regional strategic plan that becomes the guide for regional policy is created as a byproduct of:

1. the regional vision and
2. the current regional reality.

A flaw in step one and two will result in a flawed regional plan and flawed polices.

A GIANT OF STRATEGIC VISION

Born in Singapore to a wealthy Chinese family, Lee Kuan Yew was educated at Fitzwilliam College, Cambridge, and was called to the bar at Middle Temple. Upon return to Singapore he became an advocate and solicitor, and in 1954 founded the moderately anti-Communist People's Action Party whose general secretary he remained until 1992. Lee Kuan Yew was elected to the Singapore Legislative Assembly in 1955. He became the country's first Prime Minister in 1959, and was re-elected in 1963, 1968, 1972, 1976, 1980, 1984, and 1988. He resigned in November 1990.

Today Singapore's *per capita* income is second only to that of Japan, and the state has no foreign debts. Lee Kuan Yew's creation, modern Singapore, is an economic powerhouse. With one of the world's highest *per capita* incomes, high-quality schools, health care and public services it is a magnet for global labor.

In an interview with *International Herald Tribune, Yew* talked about the ideological framework that guided his strategy for making his vision of a "first-world oasis in a third-world region" a reality. Singapore's "secret," Lee said, is that it is "ideology free" – an unsentimental pragmatism that fuses the workings of the country as if it were in itself an ideology. "Does it work?" Lee said. "Let's try it and if it does work, fine, let's continue it. If it doesn't work, toss it out, try another one." The yardstick, he said, is the question, "Is this necessary for survival and progress? If it is, let's do it."

"To understand Singapore," Yew maintains, "you've got to start…with an improbable story: It should not exist." He describes it as a nation with almost no natural resources, a mix of Chinese, Malay and Indian cultures where everyone relies on the country's "wits to stay afloat and prosper…. We built up the infrastructure. The difficult part was getting the people to change their habits so they behaved more like first world citizens, not like third world citizens spitting and littering all over the place."

Smart, regional strategy involves doing what is required within your set of ethical values to accomplish the regional vision, while not becoming a prisoner of the ideologies of the various political schools of thought.

CHAPTER FIVE

LEADERSHIP JUDGMENT

Judgment is the ability to judge or make decisions objectively, authoritatively, and wisely. It is the forming of an opinion, estimate, notion, or conclusion, from circumstances presented to the mind.

Good judgment in any realm of life is based on two factors:

- understanding strategic interests
- having quality information

Good judgment is always necessary, but even more so in political leadership where the perils of bad decision-making could cost lives, regional treasure and people's livelihoods.

Your judgment in the following key areas will define your political legacy:

- concerning the strategic direction of your region
- during times of crisis
- in the staff you appoint
- in crafting social, economic, foreign and regional security policy

- in campaigning and securing your political future

JUDGMENT CONCERNING STRATEGIC DIRECTION

The vision, strategic objectives, goals and tactics of a region are the product of a leader's judgment. When they do not reflect the potential and current reality of the nation, failure is inevitable.

Personal Application

Who is your model of a great political strategist in the area of governance and why?

_____

_____

_____

_____

_____

_____

JUDGMENT DURING TIMES OF CRISIS

Regional crises and political leadership are inseparable because we live in a world where natural, social, economic and military disaster is always around the corner. Right judgment will either minimize or magnify a crisis.

National Crisis Thinking Model:

Let's examine a thinking model for crisis management.

1.   *Find out what is really going on.*

Seek an accurate diagnosis of the problem to discover its roots and fruit. This diagnosis, depending on the nature of the problem, will involve intensive dialogue with representatives of the following entities:

- Personal brain trust
- Intelligence services
- Foreign governments
- International agencies

2.   *Find out what can be controlled and what's outside your control.*

This information is crucial. It establishes the parameters for the steps you will have take to solve the problem. Is the problem outside your control? If so, can you control it indirectly by relating with other nations, entities and organizations? For example, natural disasters such as hurricanes and volcano's are impossible for political administrations to control. Is it a man- made problem? Man made problems, I believe, can be solved by men working in synergy with men.

3.   *Discern what outcome will be considered successful for your region.*

This step is important because it guides a swift response. When this step is not in place, actions tend to be haphazard and fail to produce a satisfactory outcome.

4.   *Generate ideas to produce a successful outcome.*

This is the creative step and it requires for you and your brain-trust to generate multiple ideas to solve the problem. At this point you will not yet choose a solution.

> 5. *Choose a workable solution within your realm of control.*

This is the stage where you narrow down your options and choose a solution from the lists of ideas you have generated.

> 6. *Activate the response.*

This is the final step when you align the resources of your administration in single focus to solve the problem.

Personal Application

1. Describe the best example of a political leader who solved a major crisis by thinking well.

_____

_____

_____

_____

_____

_____

_____

_____

_____

_____

_____

2. Describe the best example of a political leader who turned a crisis into a regional disaster by his approach in solving a problem.

_____

_____

_____

_____

_____

_____

_____

_____

_____

_____

_____

_____

JUDGMENT IN THE APPOINTMENT OF STAFF

People are like escalators; they will either take you up or down. Your staff can make or break you. Those closest to a leader determine the leader's level of success. A leader who makes the judgment to assemble a team of loyal and able advisors and staff has significantly increased his chances of notable success.

Personal Application

Give an example of an exceptionally gifted political leader who failed to achieve his notable vision because of an inner circle of incompetent and disloyal staff and advisors he had appointed.

_____
_____
_____
_____
_____
_____
_____
_____
_____
_____
_____

JUDGMENT IN CRAFTING SOCIAL, ECONOMIC, FOREIGN AND REGIONAL

SECURITY POLICY

In the areas of social, economic, foreign and national security policy, hundreds of policy prescriptions have been created by experts who have advised the leader based on their contradictory, scholarly opinions representing different schools of thought. One of the most important judgment calls, therefore, is for the leader to choose policies from among the extensive menu of contradictory opinions that will realize the regional vision and its strategic objectives.

Personal Application

Give an example of different schools of thought expressed by world-renowned experts in the area of growing national economies.

_____

_____

_____

_____

_____

_____

_____

_____

_____

_____

_____

JUDGMENT IN CAMPAIGNING AND SECURING A POLITICAL FUTURE

Campaigning and political leadership are inseparable. Your judgments in this area will affect the tenure and scope of your political leadership.

Personal Application

What is required to swing the vote in your favor in the next election?

_____

_____

LEADERSHIP JUDGEMENT

CHAPTER SIX

ONE GREAT LEADER
IS NOT ENOUGH

Critical mass scientifically refers to the smallest amount of fissile material needed for a sustained nuclear chain reaction.

The principle of critical mass is applicable to the transformation of a country. A small, critical mass of passionate and competent people, both in the administration and the general population, is required to drive a sustained transformation. This catalytic group influences the direction of the nation, and the general population mostly follows their lead.

I have observed these political equations in nations:

1. *Willing and competent leader + unwilling and unskilled people creates a frustrated leader*

2. *Unwilling and unskilled leader + willing and competent people creates a frustrated population*

3. *Unwilling and unskilled leader + unwilling and unskilled people creates a failed state*

4. *Willing and unskilled leader + willing and competent people creates a struggling state*

   ☐

5. *Willing and competent leader + willing and competent people \favorable circumstance creates a growing nation with a great economy*

Personal Application

Which political equations have been in operation in the last four successive administrations in your nation?

_____

_____

_____

_____

_____

_____

_____

_____

_____

_____

_____

_____

PASSION AND ABILITY

In an analysis to determine whether there is a critical mass in the administration and the general population for influencing national transformation, it is necessary to focus on the key areas of passion and ability.

1. **Passion in the administration:** There is no gap like a passion-gap between a political leader and his administration! It is the birth place of significant frustration, and if unresolved, will be the tomb of your visions and plans.

A sustained passion gap between a leader and his staff is only solved by firing and rehiring passionate and competent staff.

Personal Application

Give an example from your experience of a passion gap between a political leader and the members of his administration.

_____

_____

_____

_____

_____

_____

_____

_____

_____

_____

_____

_____

Passion in the General Population: A passion gap between a leader and his citizens for national growth is a stiffer challenge. The prescription for this aliment can only be applied after a thorough diagnostic process has been carried out and a strategy for igniting patriotism in the nation has been identified.

Patriotism is emotional capital that can make the difference in the transformation process.

When patriotism is awakened and focused by a wise leader, it motivates people to desire to sacrifice for the national good.

Personal Application

Give a historical example of how a political leader ignited patriotism that caused people to sacrifice for their national freedom, growth or transformation.

_____

_____

_____

_____

_____

_____

_____

_____

_____

_____

_____

2. **Ability in the Administration:** Ability is a must. It is central to realizing national vision. National vision has an ability threshold for its fulfillment and requirements must be clearly understood. Cronyism, the practice of favoring one's close friends, especially with political appointments, won't work particularly when the friends are unskilled. Cronyism will sabotage your vision and might even erode trust in your leadership.

A lack of ability among the administration can only be solved by training people who have potential and hiring those who are competent.

Personal Application

Give a historical example how a political administration failed its constituents through cronyism.

_____

_____

_____

_____

_____

_____

_____

_____

_____

_____

3.   **Ability in the General Population:** A lack of required skills among the general population can only be solved by the strategic mobilization of national resources to educate the masses.

Personal Application

Give a historical example how a political leader achieved economic growth by successfully mobilizing national resources to empower his constituents through education.

_____

_____

_____

_____

_____

_____

_____

_____

_____

_____

CHAPTER SEVEN

CULTURAL INTELLIGENCE

LEADERSHIP

Cultural intelligence is the ability and skill to understand, influence and achieve positive results within a distinct culture.

Cultural intelligence is one of the missing links in creating good policies and applying the principles of good governance in developing nations and regions. An excellent model of governance and policy making is based on two foundations:

- Sound principles
- Cultural realities

The lack of cultural intelligence dooms many supposed solutions for developing regions to failure. Such solutions may contain sound principles, but they are applied in a culturally contrary way. It is important to recognize that political leadership at its highest level is not a science, but a cultural art form. It involves application of the pillars of:

- Political vision
- Leadership character

- Political strategy
- Sound political judgment
- The building of a critical mass of passionate and competent people
in
  a way that reflects the strengths and weakness of the culture.

Fareed Zakaria an article titled, *Culture Is Destiny; A Conversation with Lee Kuan Yew*, records this conversation:

Fareed Zakaria: *If culture is so important, then countries with very different cultures may not, in fact, succeed in the way that East Asia did by getting economic fundamentals right. Are you not hopeful for the countries around the world that are liberalizing their economies?*

Lee Kuan Yew: *Getting the fundamentals right would help, but these societies will not succeed in the same way as East Asia did because certain driving forces will be absent. If you have a culture that doesn't place much value in learning and scholarship and hard work and thrift and deferment of present enjoyment for future gain, the going will be much slower.*
But, you know, the World Bank report's conclusions are part of the culture of America, and by extension, of international institutions. It had to present its findings in a bland and universalizable way, which I find unsatisfying because it doesn't grapple with the real problems. It makes the hopeful assumption that all men are equal, that people all over the world are the same. They are not. I believe that due to the ever-blowing winds of positive and negative change in our culture, the next generation of political leaders must develop their cultural intelligence.

Personal Application

Give an example of a great policy that was applied in a culturally unintelligent way causing it to fail to produce the intended effect.

_____

_____

_____

_____

_____

_____

_____

_____

_____

_____

_____

_____

Five Aspects of Cultural Intelligence

1. **Understanding the culture:** Understanding the inherent and sometimes evolving culture of the region you desire to lead is a fundamental requirement for political leaders in today's world. Culture is based upon the arts, beliefs and institutions of a population that are passed down from generation to generation. It is rightly called "the way of life" of an entire society. As such, it encompasses codes of manner and dress, language, religious beliefs, rituals, norms of behavior (including

laws and morality), systems of belief and various art forms. Culture directly influences how people respond to political leaders' policies and models of governance. It bears repetition that **all successful models of governance and policies in countries are based on solid principles with a distinct cultural flavor.**

It is also a reality that different ethnic groups and regions within the nation have their own unique subculture. An understanding of these subcultures increases a leader's prospects of succeeding significantly.

Personal Application

Describe the culture of your region.

_____

_____

_____

_____

_____

_____

_____

_____

_____

_____

_____

_____

2. **Understanding the winds of change within the culture:** The advent of the Internet, easy worldwide travel and globalization have created a distinctive era in human civilization. It's the era of access to information. There has never been a time in the history of the world when men and women can, from the comfort of their homes, or an Internet café, access and interact with the virtues and vices of every culture under heaven. This access to information always precipitates changes and behavior that leads to shifts in cultural norms. Political leaders must be observers and students of emerging trends produced in this era of access to information.

Personal Application

In your region, how does access to information affect the culture?

_____

_____

_____

_____

_____

_____

_____

_____

_____

_____

_____

3. **Influencing culture:** To influence culture you must:
    · Understand the style of leadership that produces results.
    · Know whether your region's cultural goal posts are moving.

What should you do? Know the culture of your people. The people you want to lead politically merit your comprehensive study.

    · Study the history of your nation to determine how its successful and unsuccessful leaders operated
    · Study what it takes to emotionally connect with your culture

It is always necessary to move the heart before you can move the hand or the head.

Personal Application

Give an example of a political leader who changed his style of leadership to connect emotionally with a cultural group.

_____
_____
_____
_____
_____
_____
_____
_____
_____

5. **Defending your culture from negative influences:** Our era of access to information has carried many nations on the wings of progress to positive change. It has also injected them with the sewage of immorality and diabolical behavior that, if left unchecked, can erode the strengths of many cultures.

An institution at the foundation of all human progress that has stood the test of time, is **the family.** The institution of the family consists of a man, his wife and his children. It has been the fountain of human civilization since recorded time. The family is now under attack. Anything that seeks to erode or undermine this basic unit of society represents a step backward in social order.

No institution, program, policy, or alternate model ever created has been able to duplicate the power of the family unit to raise the next generation. That power of family lies in the loving commitment of a husband and wife to each other, and their willingness to sacrifice and invest in the future of their children.

Personal Application

Give examples of attempts to undermine the place and value of the traditional family in your region.

_____

_____

_____

_____

_____

_____

_____

_____

_____

5.   **Achieving Results Positively:** Great political leaders are culturally aware and know when cultural re-engineering for the benefit of society is a necessity. They are focused on developing the next generation into citizens who contribute positively to their communities and nation. Great political leaders seeking their nation's progress protect the next generation from regressive cultural re-engineering.

CHAPTER EIGHT

WHERE DO WE GO FROM HERE?

I have shared with you leadership concepts and taken you on a journey of understanding the mechanics of implementing a political vision.

As you apply these principles, always remember that all great leaders:

- Understand themselves
- Are clear on what they want to achieve.
- Understand the culture of the people they lead.

These, in my opinion, are the key differences between good and great political leaders.

The more you grow in political leadership wisdom, the more you will increase in your ability to overcome challenges and seize opportunities existent in your national culture, geography, circumstances and legacy.

Nations are crying out for transformational political leadership.

I see you rising to the challenge!

REFERENCES

**Chapter
One**

Address by the Rt. Hon. Owen Arthur, Prime Minister, on the occasion of the unveiling of the statue of the Right Excellent Errol Barrow – National Hero, Independence Square, January 21, 2007. Prime Minister's Office

**Chapter
Three**

Interview with Nelson Mandela. *Newsweek*, July 7, 2008.

**Chapter
Four**

Interview with Lee Kuan Yew. *International Herald Tribune*, August 29,
20
07.

**Chapter
Five**

Think Better: An Innovator's Guide to Productive Thinking. Hurson, Tim. **McGraw-Hill Books 2006**

**Chapter
Seven**

Culture Is Destiny: A Conversation with Lee Kuan Yew. Zakaria, Fareed.
Zakaria. March/April, 1994 Foreign Affairs

ABOUT THE AUTHOR

Andre Thomas is a strategic executive consultant for individuals, businesses, non-profit organizations and governments around the world.

As a writer and coach for visionaries, Andre brings to bear a profound understanding of ancient wisdom on contemporary challenges, to identify and articulate "destiny "DNA"-launching institutions and individuals from the first steps of identifying fundamental strengths, values and goals to accomplished greatness.

As an identity and strategy consultant, Andre has trained hundreds of emerging and renowned business, social, organizational and political leaders. His seminars have included participants from the United Nations, NGOs, government agencies and the private business, education, health and arts/entertainment sectors.

He is the founder and thought leader of The Ideas & Solutions Group

Our website: www.ideasandsolutions.org

The
IDEAS & SOLUTIONS
Group

Purpose

To equip a critical mass of leaders in nations to bring ideas and solutions from concept to reality through the principles and process of transformational leadership and economic dignity

Mission

To work through strategic partnerships and use events, coaching, media, resources and consulting to create leadership wisdom culture in organizations and nations that takes ideas and solutions from concept to reality

Vision

To see transformation occur in nations and their economies as leaders emerge who bring ideas and solutions from concept to reality.

Philosophy

1. The problems of a generation will never be greater than the ideas and solutions within people born into that generation
2. These ideas and solutions are within people in the form of an uncommon vision
3. Leadership wisdom is applying principles and taking steps to take ideas and solutions from concept to reality
4. Except the leadership wisdom operating the visionary matches the scope of the vision, the uncommon vision within them will not be fulfilled

Website

www.ideasandsolutions.org

OTHER BOOKS
BY ANDRE THOMAS

Unlock Your Greatness (A Young Leaders Handbook)

Uncommon Men and Distinguished Women
(A Rites of Passage Handbook for Young Men and Women)

The Gift of Organizational Leadership

www.ingramcontent.com/pod-product-compliance
Lightning Source LLC
Chambersburg PA
CBHW071233290326
41931CB00037B/2871